REAL LIFE SEA MONSTERS

Box Jellyfish

by Ruth Owen

PowerKiDS press™

New York

Published in 2014 by The Rosen Publishing Group, Inc.
29 East 21st Street, New York, NY 10010

Produced for Rosen by Ruby Tuesday Books Ltd
Editor for Ruby Tuesday Books Ltd: Mark J. Sachner
US Editor: Joshua Shadowens
Designer: Emma Randall

Photo Credits:
Cover, 1, 8–9, 18–19, 26–27 © FLPA; 4–5, 12–13, 14–15 © National
Geographic Creative; 6–7, 16, 20–21 © Shutterstock; 10–11, 28–29 ©
OceanWideImages; 17, 19 © Superstock; 22–23 © Public Domain;
24–25 © 2013 Ned DeLoach.

Library of Congress Cataloging-in-Publication Data

Owen, Ruth, 1967– author.
 Box jellyfish / Ruth Owen.
     pages cm. — (Real life sea monsters)
 Includes index.
 ISBN 978-1-4777-6270-7 (library binding) — ISBN 978-1-4777-6269-1 (pbk.) —
 ISBN 978-1-4777-6271-4 (6-pack)
 1. Cubomedusae—Juvenile literature. 2. Jellyfishes—Juvenile literature.
 I. Title.
 QL377.S4O94 2014
 593.5'3–dc23

                              2013035041

Manufactured in the United States of America

CPSIA Compliance Information: Batch #W14PK7: For Further Information contact: Rosen Publishing, New York, New York at 1-800-237-9932

CONTENTS

A DEADLY ENCOUNTER

It's a beautiful day on a beach in Australia. A swimmer wades into the warm ocean water. Little does he know that just inches (cm) from his body is one of the world's most dangerous creatures.

The animal is a box jellyfish, and its **translucent** body is almost invisible. If the unsuspecting swimmer were to accidentally brush against the jellyfish's see-through **tentacles**, the animal would respond by releasing millions of **venomous** stings. Within a matter of minutes, the swimmer could be dead!

Thankfully, the jellyfish slowly moves away, and the swimmer is unaware that he has just encountered a deadly real life sea monster.

There are many different **species** of box jellyfish. The animal in the photograph is a *Chironex fleckeri* (Ki-ron-ex fleck-er-eye). It is one of the most dangerous species.

Box jellyfish

Tentacles

ALL ABOUT JELLYFISH

Jellyfish live in oceans worldwide, but they are not actually **fish**. Jellyfish are **invertebrates** that belong to a group of animals called **cnidarians**. This animal group also includes creatures such as corals and sea anemones.

Jellyfish have no bones, heart, or brain, and are made mostly of water. They have a main body part called a bell and long tentacles. Jellyfish species that scientists call "true jellyfish" have umbrella-shaped bells. Box jellyfish species have box or cube-shaped bells that give these animals their name.

Some box jellyfish species have many tentacles hanging from each of the four corners of their bells. Other box jellyfish species have just one tentacle on each corner.

A sea nettle "true jellyfish"

Umbrella-shaped bell

Tentacles

Tentacle

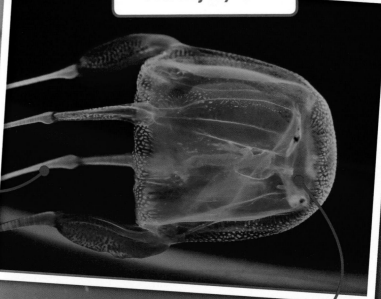

A box jellyfish

Cube-shaped bell

The stings of some types of box jellyfish cause only a mild pain. The stings of other species, however, can be agonizing and even **fatal**!

MEET A DEADLY JELLYFISH

The deadly *Chironex fleckeri* box jellyfish is a species with many tentacles.

The bell of this type of box jellyfish can grow to the size of a basketball. On each corner of the bell, the animal has a bunch of thick, flat tentacles. There may be as many as 15 tentacles on each corner.

The jellyfish can contract its tentacles so they are just a few inches (cm) long. When the animal is moving through the ocean, however, it extends its tentacles behind it. Then the tentacles may reach nearly 10 feet (3 m) long.

A *Chironex fleckeri* jellyfish has four sense organs. The organs can detect light and dark and vibrations in the water made by possible predators.

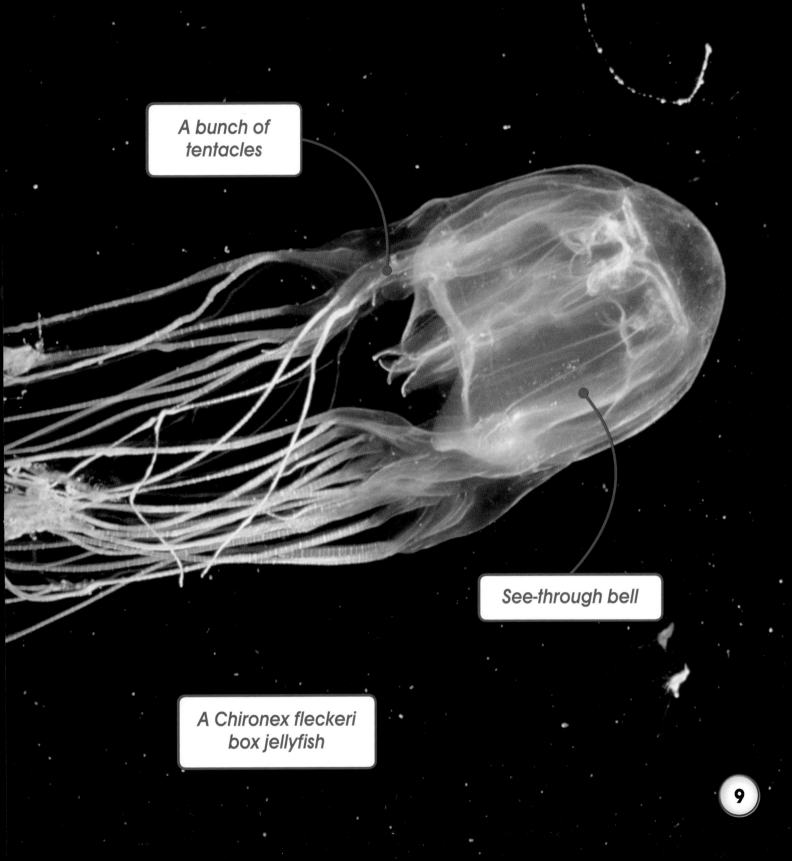

A bunch of
tentacles

See-through bell

A Chironex fleckeri
box jellyfish

9

THE BIG STINGER

The name of the *Chironex fleckeri* box jellyfish comes from the Greek word *cheiro*, which means "hand," and the **Latin** word *nex*, which means "murderer."

The word *fleckeri* comes from Dr. Hugo Flecker, a scientist involved in studying this jellyfish. The animal's everyday, common names give us the biggest clue, however, as to why this creature is so dangerous. In Australia, people call this type of box jellyfish the sea wasp, the big stinger, and the sea stinger.

The jellyfish's long tentacles have millions of special **cells**. Each of these cells contains a tiny stinging dart called a **nematocyst**. Each microscopic dart is loaded with a powerful dose of killer **venom**.

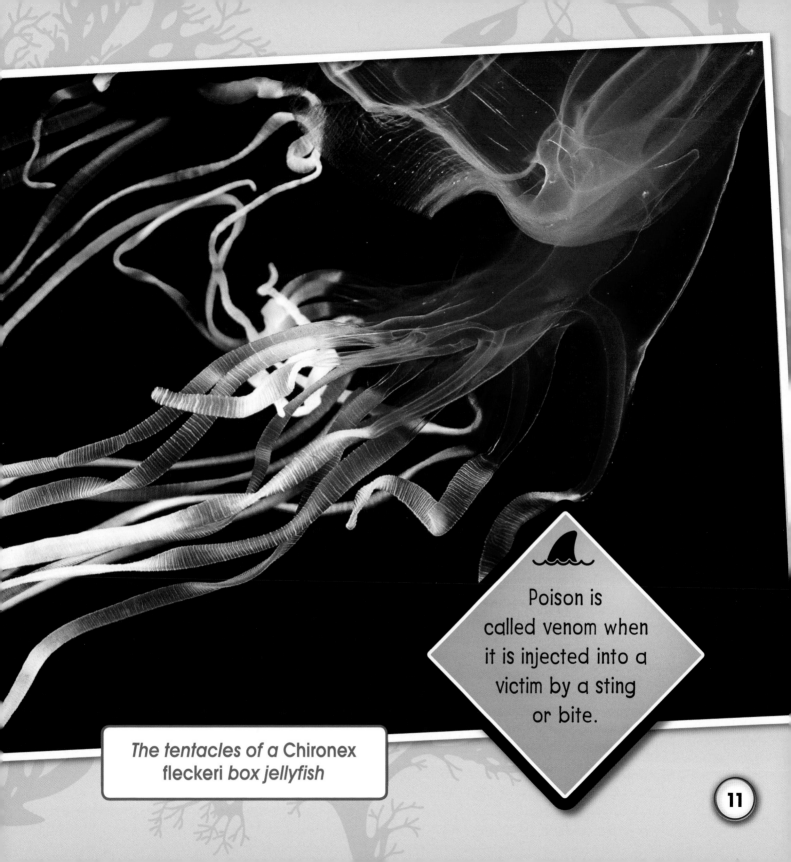

The tentacles of a Chironex fleckeri box jellyfish

Poison is called venom when it is injected into a victim by a sting or bite.

MILLIONS OF STINGS

A scientist once estimated that there might be 4,000 million, or 4 billion, nematocysts on the tentacles of a *Chironex fleckeri* box jellyfish.

If the animal has 60 tentacles, and each tentacle measures 10 feet (3 m) long, that means it has 600 feet (180 m) of tentacles. If you divide 4,000 million by 600 feet (180 m), it gives you a number of 6 million. This means that one foot (30 cm) of tentacle would contain 6 million nematocysts.

When the jellyfish's tentacle touches an animal or person's skin, chemicals on the skin cause the nematocysts to inject their venom. So just one foot (30 cm) of tentacle touching a victim's skin would deliver 6 million doses of deadly venom!

This fish has been stung by the jellyfish's tentacles and will now be eaten.

Once a box
jellyfish's tentacle
makes contact with its
victim's skin, the nematocysts
fire and inject their
venom in less than
a second.

STINGS FOR ATTACK AND DEFENSE

The deadly stings of a box jellyfish are the way in which the animal kills its prey.

A box jellyfish hunts, or fishes for prey, by moving through the water with its tentacles trailing behind it. Prey, such as fish and shrimp, touch or become entangled in the tentacles. The animals are then quickly killed by the jellyfish's stings and are pulled into the jellyfish's mouth, which is at the base of its bell.

It's important for a box jellyfish to have fast-acting venom so it can kill its prey quickly. This stops the struggling prey animal from breaking off one of its captor's tentacles.

Box jellyfish also defend themselves by stinging predators that want a meal of jellyfish!

A hawksbill turtle

Unfortunately for box jellyfish, their venomous stings have no effect on sea turtles, and sea turtles like to eat jellyfish!

A Chironex fleckeri box jellyfish

HUMANS AND BOX JELLYFISH

The deadly *Chironex fleckeri* box jellyfish does not deliberately attack humans. Sometimes, however, swimmers and jellyfish accidentally touch with horrifying consequences.

People who have been stung by this jellyfish describe an excruciating pain that feels as if their skin has been branded with red-hot irons. The tentacle marks look as if the victim has been whipped.

If a victim has tentacles still clinging to his or her skin, the tentacles may contain nematocysts that haven't fired. Pouring vinegar over these tentacles stops the remaining nematocysts from stinging.

If a huge dose of venom from many stings enters a person's body, however, the victim's heart might stop. In these severe cases, paramedics must get to the victim within minutes.

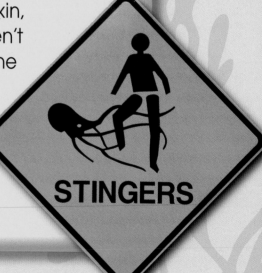

STINGERS

Scientists are still studying where *Chironex fleckeri* live. They are regularly found in waters around Australia, and have been found in other parts of the Pacific Ocean.

On beaches close to areas where box jellyfish are found, warning signs are put up. Vinegar is also supplied as a first aid treatment.

STINGERS
ESENT
WATERS

✚ VINEGAR
For use on MARINE STINGS
POUR ON - DO NOT RUB
SEEK MEDICAL ATTENTION

A LUCKY ESCAPE

On a Sunday in April 2011, seven-year-old Osbourne Kewe was spending time in the ocean at Pallarenda Beach in Townsville, Queensland, Australia.

Suddenly, the air was filled with the little boy's terrible screams. Osbourne had been badly stung by a box jellyfish. In unbelievable agony, Osbourne was pulled from the sea by his older sister and other beachgoers.

Then, just as suddenly, there was silence. Osbourne had stopped breathing. In an amazing stroke of luck, nurse Kim Riley was walking her dogs on the beach. Kim realized what had happened and immediately began to give Osbourne **CPR**.

As everyone waited for paramedics to arrive, Kim had to restart Osbourne's heart twice. Thanks to her quick thinking, however, Osbourne survived his horrifying ordeal.

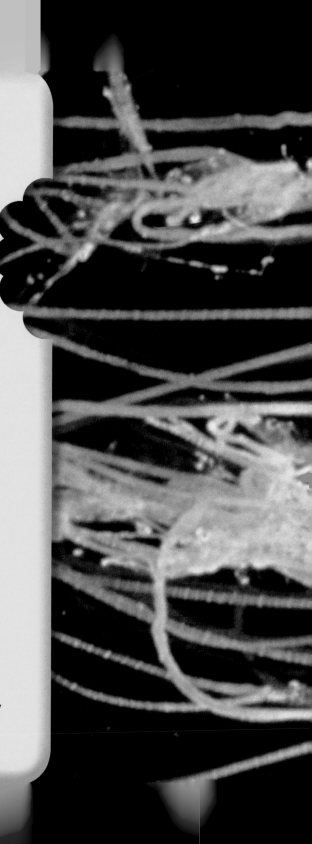

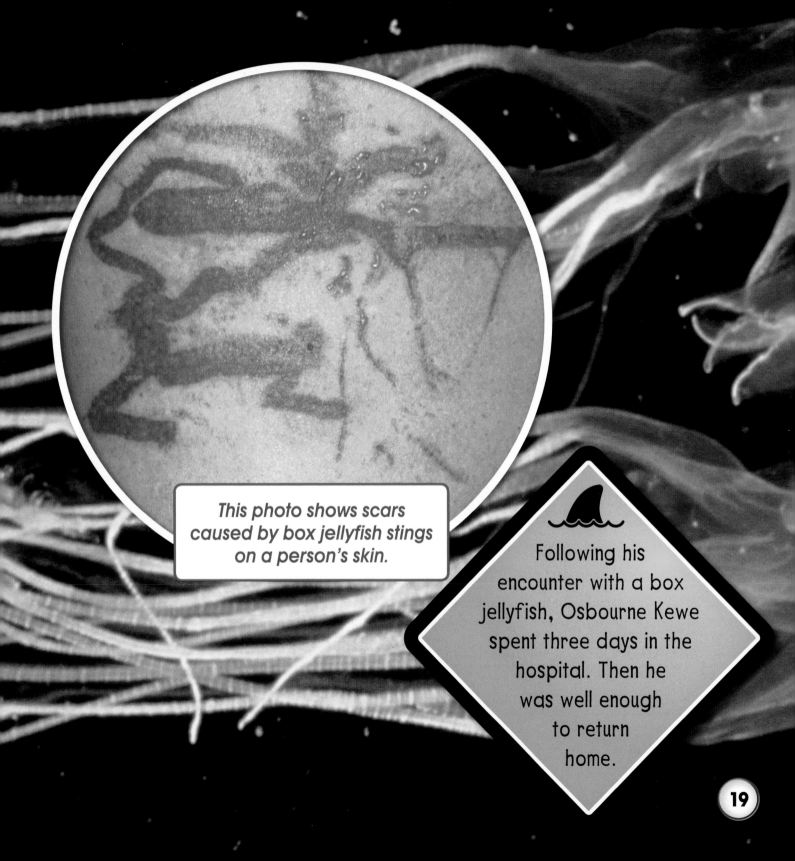

This photo shows scars caused by box jellyfish stings on a person's skin.

Following his encounter with a box jellyfish, Osbourne Kewe spent three days in the hospital. Then he was well enough to return home.

TINY, INVISIBLE STINGERS

When swimming in a warm ocean off the coast of Australia, swimmers might occasionally wonder if a shark or other large, wild creature is close by.

Little do these unsuspecting humans realize that they are sharing the water with an animal far more terrifying than a shark. That's because these waters are home to tiny, see-through box jellyfish that are about the size of a dime!

These miniscule, but deadly, animals are known as Irukandji jellyfish. These creatures may be small, but anyone stung by one of them quickly learns that an encounter with an Irukandji box jellyfish can be horrifying.

This beautiful, warm ocean water could contain a venomous creature so tiny a swimmer won't even know it's there.

The name "Irukandji" is a group name for several species of tiny, venomous box jellyfish. Scientists still have lots to learn about these animals.

IRUKANDJI SYNDROME

Scientists are still **classifying** the different types of Irukandji box jellyfish. What they do know, however, is that members of this group can cause a terrifying condition known as Irukandji syndrome.

Stings from Irukandji jellyfish are often not that painful. Sometimes a person doesn't even realize he or she has been stung. Then, after about 30 minutes, the horror begins.

First, the victim develops severe back pains. Then painful cramps spread through the person's arms, legs, and chest. The victim will vomit and be drenched in sweat. His or her heart will beat faster and blood pressure will rise.

In very severe cases, sufferers of Irukandji syndrome have died. Thankfully, with medical treatment most victims survive.

Irukandji box jellyfish have cube-shaped bells and just one tentacle on each corner of the bell.

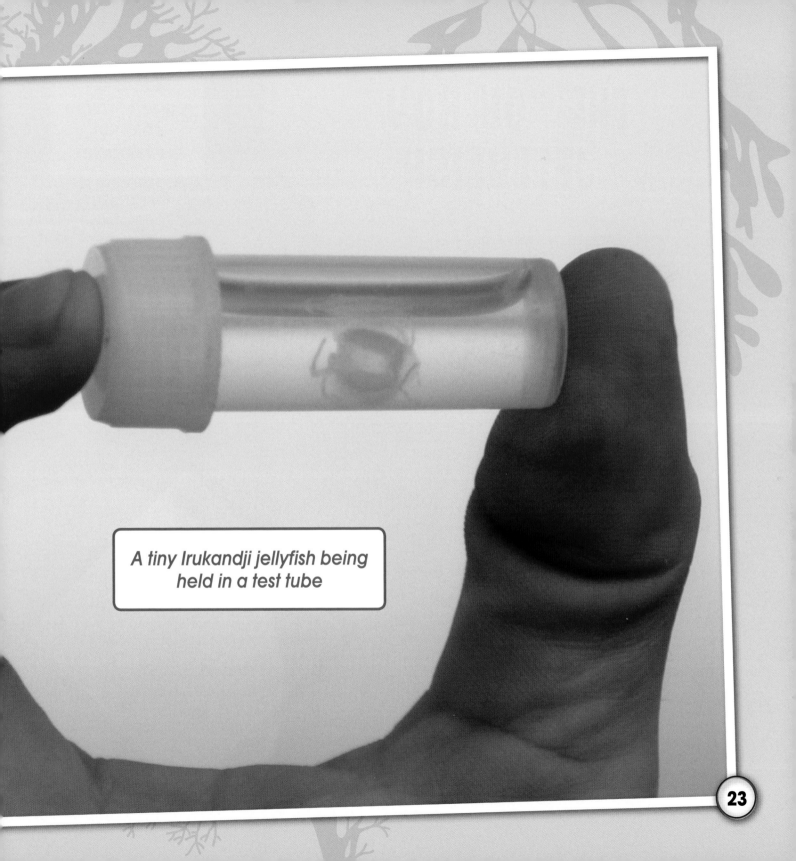

A tiny Irukandji jellyfish being held in a test tube

THE "OH BOY" JELLYFISH

In 2011, scientists officially classified and named a new species of box jellyfish.

The Bonaire banded box jellyfish was discovered off the coast of the Caribbean island of Bonaire. This fast-swimming jellyfish is highly venomous.

In order to give the new species its scientific name, an online naming competition was set up by a science organization in the United States.

The competition was won by the name *Tamoya ohboya*. It was thought up by a US biology teacher named Lisa Peck. The name comes from "Tamoyidae," which is the jellyfish's scientific family name, and "Oh Boy." That's what Lisa thinks is probably the first thing people say when they see this beautiful creature!

The *Tamoya ohboya* box jellyfish has a bell covered with warts. The jellyfish's tentacles and warts can deliver painful stings.

Wart-covered bell

The Caribbean Island of Bonaire

THE LION'S MANE JELLYFISH

The lion's mane jellyfish is a species of "true jellyfish." Like its box jellyfish cousins, however, this ocean giant can deliver painful stings.

The bell of a lion's mane jellyfish can grow to over 6 feet (2 m) across. Its stinging tentacles can stretch for many feet (m).

In July 2010, a lion's mane jellyfish stung about 100 people at the Wallis Sands State Park beach in Rye, New Hampshire. It's believed that the jellyfish was actually dead. As the animal was washed toward the beach, however, its tentacles broke up and were still able to deliver thousands of painful stings to people who were in the water!

A lion's mane jellyfish

This jellyfish gets its name from the mass of long, hair-like tentacles that look like a lion's mane.

Lion's mane jellyfish usually live in northern seas and cool, northern regions of the Atlantic and Pacific Ocean.

STAYING SAFE

Hawaiian scientist Dr. Angel Yanagihara wants to help the victims of box jellyfish stings. And for Angel, it's personal!

On an early morning swim, Angel swam into a swarm of tiny Irukandji jellyfish. She suffered agonizing stings over much of her body and became very ill. Now, Angel studies the poisons in box jellyfish venom and develops drugs to combat their effects on humans.

In places where box jellyfish live, swimmers should always look out for jellyfish warning signs. People can also protect their skin with a wet suit or some other kind of protective clothing, even panty hose. Box jellyfish are just doing what comes naturally. So it's up to humans to stay safe when they dive into the world of the box jellyfish!

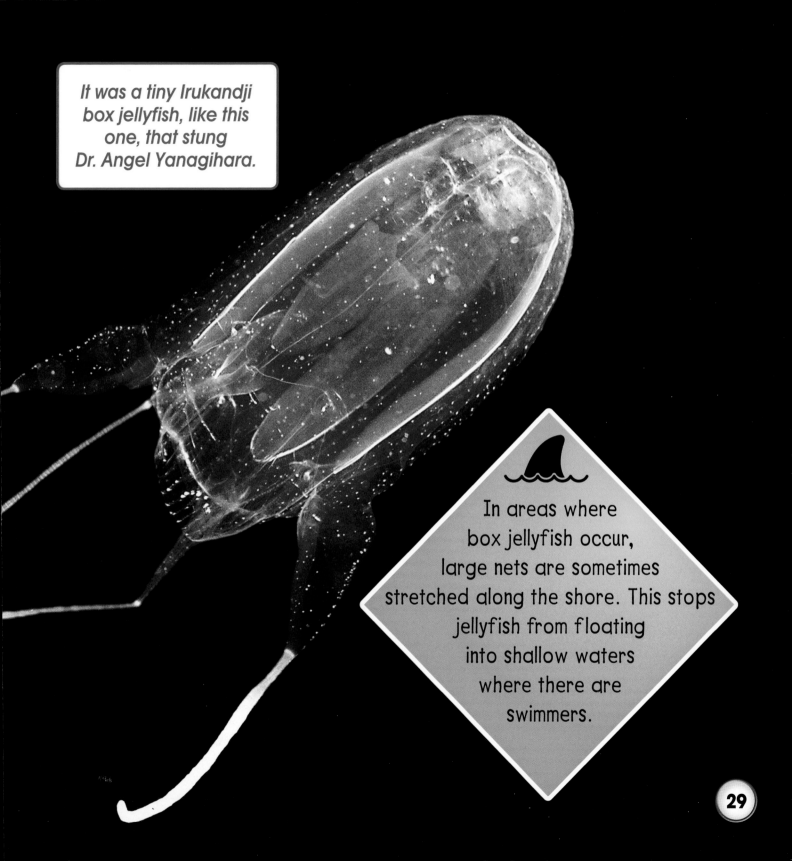

It was a tiny Irukandji box jellyfish, like this one, that stung Dr. Angel Yanagihara.

In areas where box jellyfish occur, large nets are sometimes stretched along the shore. This stops jellyfish from floating into shallow waters where there are swimmers.

29

GLOSSARY

cells (SELZ)
Very tiny parts of a living thing.

classifying (KLA-suh-fy-ing)
Sorting or arranging things in groups according to their features.

cnidarians (ny-DER-ee-unz)
Invertebrate animals, such as jellyfish, corals, and sea anemones, that live in water and have jelly-like bodies.

CPR (SEE-pee-ar)
Emergency procedures for bringing back the breathing and heartbeat of a victim of an accident or heart failure. "CPR" stands for "cardiopulmonary resuscitation."

fatal (FAY-tul)
Causing death.

fish (FISH)
Cold-blooded animals that live in water. Fish breathe through gills and have a skeleton. Most fish lay eggs.

invertebrates (in-VER-teh-brets)
Animals that have no backbone. This animal group includes ocean animals such as squid, octopuses, and jellyfish, and land animals such as insects, which have hard outer shells instead of bony skeletons, as well as worms and snails.

Latin (LA-tun)
An ancient language that developed in Italy and is still used by scientists today for naming living things.

nematocyst (NEH-muh-tuh-sist)
A cell that contains a tiny stinging dart that delivers a dose of venom.

predators (PREH-duh-turz)
Animals that hunt and kill other animals for food.

prey (PRAY)
An animal this is hunted by another animal as food.

species (SPEE-sheez)
One type of living thing. The members of a species look alike and can produce young together.

tentacles (TEN-tih-kulz)
Long body parts that some animals can use like arms.

translucent (tranz-LOO-sunt)
Clear or partly see-through.

venom (VEH-num)
A poisonous substance passed by one animal into another through a bite or sting.

venomous (VEH-nuh-mus)
Using venom, or poison, as a means of attack or defense. The venom is injected into a victim through a sting or bite.

WEBSITES

Due to the changing nature of Internet links, PowerKids Press has developed an online list of websites related to the subject of this book. This site is updated regularly. Please use this link to access the list:

www.powerkidslinks.com/rlsm/jelly/

READ MORE

Chesire, Gerard, and David Salariya. *Jellyfish*. Scary Creatures. New York: Scholastic, 2008.

Metz, Lorijo. *Discovering Jellyfish*. Along the Shore. New York: PowerKids Press, 2012.

Spilsbury, Louise. *Jellyfish*. A Day in the Life: Sea Animals. Mankato, MN: Heinemann, 2011.

INDEX